Samantha Moore

Easy Animals

Adult Coloring Book

For beginners, seniors and individuals with low vision

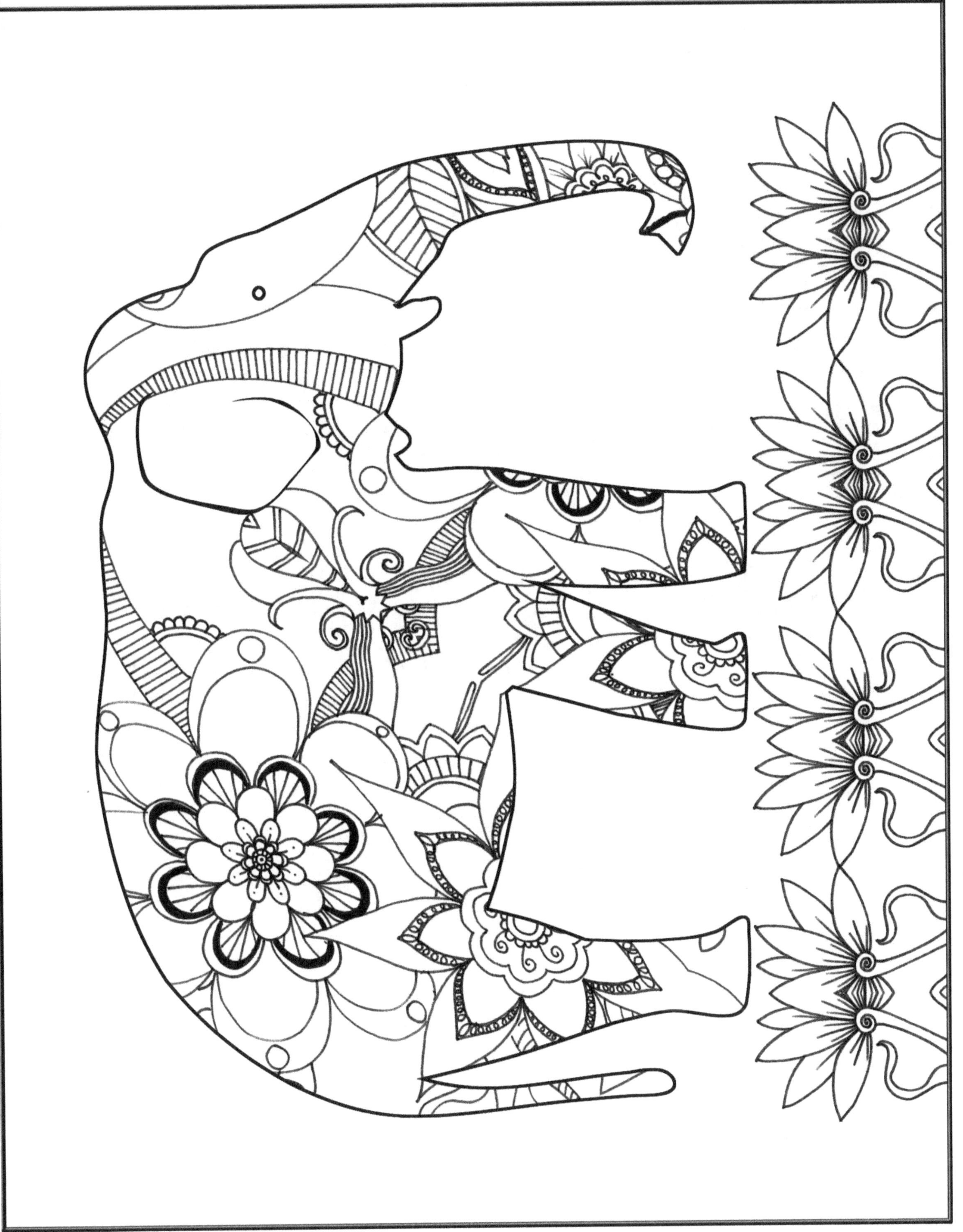

Easy Animals

Adult Coloring Book

Artist Samantha Moore loves animals and nature and this coloring book (her 6th book) is the result of her passion. Continuing with her interest in making coloring books which are simple enough to color for beginners, seniors and people with low vision or a shaky hand, Samantha has included this book in the "Easy Coloring Books" collection. In this book you will find twenty-five delightful, one sided illustrations to color as a relaxing and enjoyable pastime. The animals are designed in bolder print and some of them include some floral patterns. The objective of this book is to give you a peaceful and positive moment while coloring the designs. If you like this book, please take a moment to post a review on www.amazon.com

Enjoy.

About Samantha Moore

Since childhood artist Samantha Moore has been experimenting with colors and their influence on mood and relaxation. She has a degree in Graphic Design, a diploma in Art History and is a Reiki certified therapist.

Easy Animals - Adult coloring Book

Please feel free to contact us if you have any questions or comments:
whatacolourfulworld@mail.com

ISBN-13: 978-1985585614
ISBN-10: 1985585618

You may also like:

We would love to receive your comments. Please, find a moment to write a review.

Thank you.